#AuntAlma Unleashed

Old, Bold, and Out of Control

MORE BOOKS BY ADRIENNE ROSS

#AuntAlma: Raisin' a Little ~~Hell~~ Heaven on Earth

Push Your Way to Purpose:
How to Get from Where You Are to Where You're Meant to Be

#AuntAlma Unleashed
Old, Bold, and Out of Control

ADRIENNE ROSS

Illustrations by John Morgan

ARC Publishing

#AuntAlma Unleashed

© 2017 by Adrienne Ross

All rights reserved. No portion of this book may be reproduced, stored in a retrieval system, or transmitted in any form or by any means, electronic, mechanical, photocopying, recording, or otherwise, without the prior written permission of the publisher—except for short quotations in reviews.

Published by ARC Publishing
P.O. Box 173
Jackson, Missouri 63755

Cover design by John Morgan
Author photograph by Cheekwood Studio

Visit the author's websites: adriennerosscom.com and auntalma.com.

DEDICATION

I dedicate this book to my siblings,
Marion and Andrew.
We each have a little bit of
Aunt Alma in us.

CONTENTS

ACKNOWLEDGMENTS
INTRODUCTION
MEET ALMA ROSS, AKA #AUNTALMA

Part 1: #AuntAlma Said *What*?

Say What I Wanna
About 80 & Ain't Crazy
Long Longevity
Call Me Grandma
Wasted Workout
The Last Biscuit
Can't Complain
Get Out the Way
I Know What You Look Like
Devil in the Phone
Black as Me
Looking Good
Ugly & Pretty
Mean Folks
Lord, Have Mercy
Rude Lady

Get the Spirit & Go
Holy Spirit'll Tell You
Back of Bed
Jesus Took a Doctor
Sense and No Sense
Talking Dogs
Dog Opens Door
That Snake Got Family
How in the Hell?
Growing Old Ain't Fun
Senile…Not
Thought I'd Be Dead by Now
No Meat Receipts
Can't Steal from Yourself
Jesse James
Gimme My Money
Thief
Runnin' 'Round the Church
Wanna Go Home
Hush Yo' Mouth
Crusty Feet
Dead Leg
Wake Up 65
Teeth Don't Fit
Criminal Minds
TV Unplugged
Kung Fu Fighting
Whop Their Ass
Wedding Gift
Feelings on Sleeve

Part 2: Conversations with #AuntAlma

Jesus & Company
Ain't Staying in Here
What Time Is It There?
ATM Auntie
Ain't Scared to Die
Have Dog, Will Travel
Dirty Glasses
Fainting Auntie
Some Like It Hot
Feel It in My Bones
Ain't No Peanuts
Can't Count
Keep On Truckin'
Short & Sweet
Bingo, Anyone?
Swipe It
Let Me Count the Waves
No Time for "Hello"
Some Like It Hot
Put It in the Bowl
Bilingual Dogs

MEET THE AUTHOR
CONTACT THE AUTHOR

ACKNOWLEDGMENTS

To God be the glory. Thank You, Jesus!

Aunt Alma, thank you for being a combination of humor and wisdom. Without you, this book does not exist.

I appreciate all of my family and friends who have supported me. You have been a blessing.

John Morgan, your illustrations capture not only my aunt's words and actions, but her spirit. Thank you for bringing #AuntAlma to life.

I especially thank the *Southeast Missourian* and rustmedia. Your confidence in the first *#AuntAlma* book paved the way for this second one. I am humbled by your assistance.

INTRODUCTION

#AuntAlma is back with more side-splitting quips and quotations. "Part 1: #AuntAlma Said *What*?" offers perspectives on young adults, growing old, difficult people, and more—as only she can offer them. "Part 2: Conversations with #AuntAlma" will take you even deeper, as it reveals not only what #AuntAlma said, but what led up to what she said—the stories behind it all.

This book comes on the heels of the first *#AuntAlma book, #AuntAlma: Raisin' a Little ~~Hell~~ Heaven on Earth*. The first book gave a taste of #AuntAlma. This second book serves up a meal.

When #AuntAlma opens her mouth, we laugh. We all need to laugh more, so let's dive in. She holds nothing back here. Unleashed, she lets it fly! She is, as the title says, "Old, Bold, and Out of Control."

Meet Alma Ross, AKA #AuntAlma

Alma Louise Ross was born in Timmonsville, South Carolina, in 1937. She left the South at a young age to move to New York, but a lot of the South is still in her. She has never even lost that southern dialect. She's just combined it with New York speech and spunk, and all of it comes across in the quotations found in the two *#AuntAlma* books.

Aunt Alma was a social worker by profession, and I observed the hard work and countless hours she put into studying and writing papers to earn her bachelor's degree and then her master's degree. The year she retired from social work happened to be the year I entered the teaching profession. I saw that as a passing of the baton moment. How fitting it was that someone who had a positive effect on my education and modeled for me the rewards of hard work would reach the culmination of her career just as I commenced mine. You couldn't write it up any better than that. It fit perfectly.

Aunt Alma is one of my father's two sisters. As a child, I viewed her as the cool aunt, the lenient one, the one who came with goodies to devour. She always said things that were just as funny as they were either outrageous or wise. Some people think she developed into this hilarious character once she got up in age. Not so. For as long as I can remember, she's been good for laughs. What I love most is that she's funny without trying to be funny. She just is.

Her natural humor is how #AuntAlma gained the attention and love that led to her fame: I innocently shared on social media things she would say. She tickled everyone so much that they began requesting that I make those sayings available on mugs and T-shirts, then said I should write a book. That's how this all started. That's why she has the hashtag.

I did not mention any of this to her at first. She had no idea I was sharing her comments and actions online, did not know I had begun selling products with her words on them, and was unaware I had written a book until I published it. I'm doing the same thing with this book. I haven't said a word to her; I just take notes often as we talk on the telephone. That means that everything anyone has ever read that she has said is authentic. #AuntAlma is not scripted, practiced, or orchestrated. She's the real deal—and that's the way we love her.

PART 1:
#AUNTALMA SAID *WHAT*?

SAY WHAT I WANNA

I ain't never been in the mood for fighting. I just say what I wanna say and go on 'bout my bi'ness.

ABOUT 80 & AIN'T CRAZY

LONG LONGEVITY

CALL ME GRANDMA

My friends talk about dyeing their hair. I ain't never dyeing my hair. This gray head gets me in places I could never get into. They call me Grandma, and I love it!

WASTED WORKOUT

Them people go right outta the gym and right into that donut place, so I don't know why they even bother.

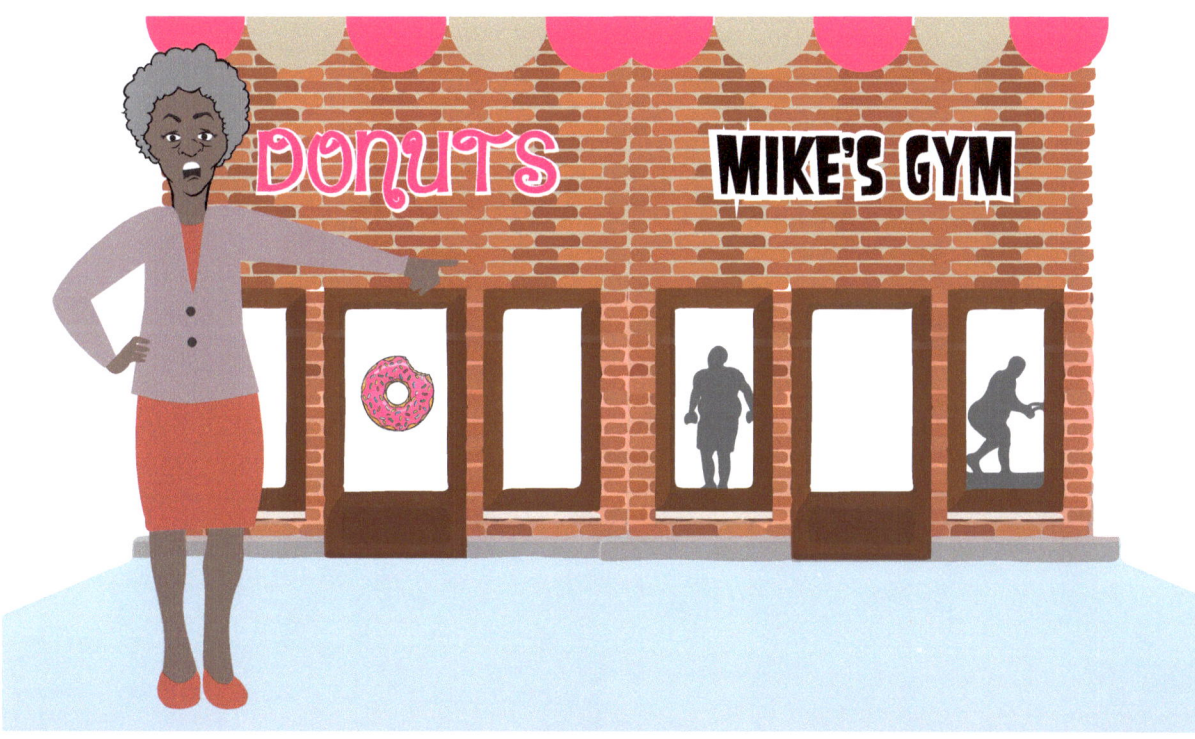

THE LAST BISCUIT

You lucky it's just 3 of y'all. Growing up, my friend had 18 brothers and sisters. Can you imagine 19 hands reaching for the last biscuit?

CAN'T COMPLAIN

I don't have time to complain. I'm too busy.

GET OUT THE WAY

I got up and got my breakfast and got in my car--and told the people to get out my way!

I KNOW WHAT YOU LOOK LIKE

DEVIL IN THE PHONE

Devil, you a liar, and a cheat, and a stinkin' dog! You know what I'm tryin' to do, and you make me hit the wrong number every time!

BLACK AS ME

LOOKING GOOD

Got on my brown and beige jacket, brown blouse, brown skirt, brown shoes, and my beige hat. I'm-a look good at church today!

UGLY & PRETTY

MEAN FOLKS

LORD, HAVE MERCY

RUDE LADY

I was 'bout to light into that rude lady. Then everybody told me how good I looked, and I wasn't 'bout to show out then. So that kept me off her behind!

HOLY SPIRIT'LL TELL YOU

When you lose something, don't jump up and down. Just sit down and ask the Holy Spirit, and He'll tell you.

BACK OF BED

JESUS TOOK A DOCTOR

SENSE & NO SENSE

TALKING DOGS

Tiny tries to talk. Shirley don't mind that she can't talk, but it bothers Tiny that *she* can't talk. I know 'cause she told me.

DOG OPENS DOOR

GROWING OLD AIN'T FUN

SENILE…NOT

I ain't senile, but I do get my days mixed up.

THOUGHT I'D BE DEAD BY NOW

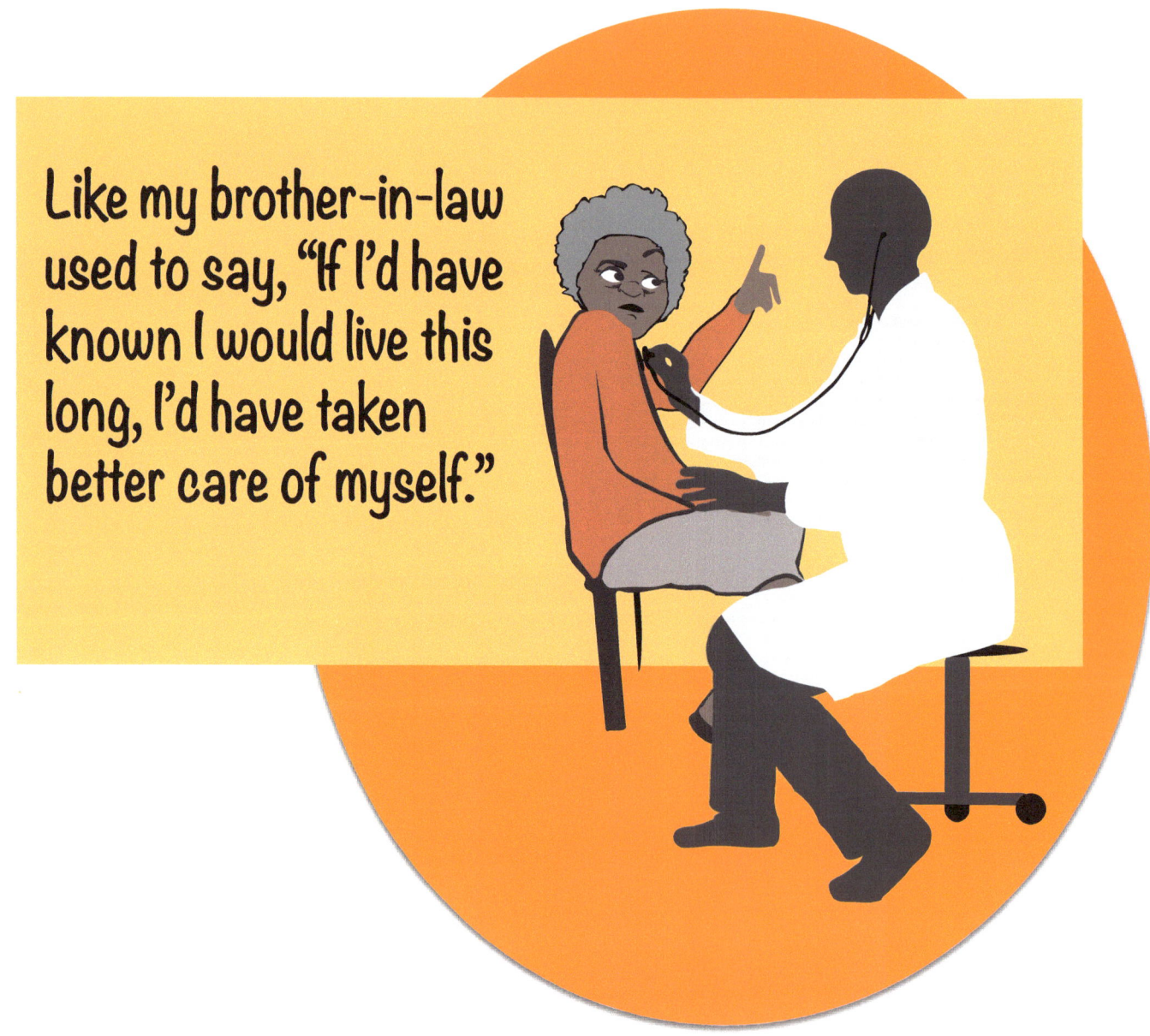

Like my brother-in-law used to say, "If I'd have known I would live this long, I'd have taken better care of myself."

NO MEAT RECEIPTS

My refrigerator I just bought done gone bad, and I had to throw out my food--and you go'n tell me I gotta prove I just bought the food before you reimburse me... Hell, I don't be keepin' no receipts for meat!

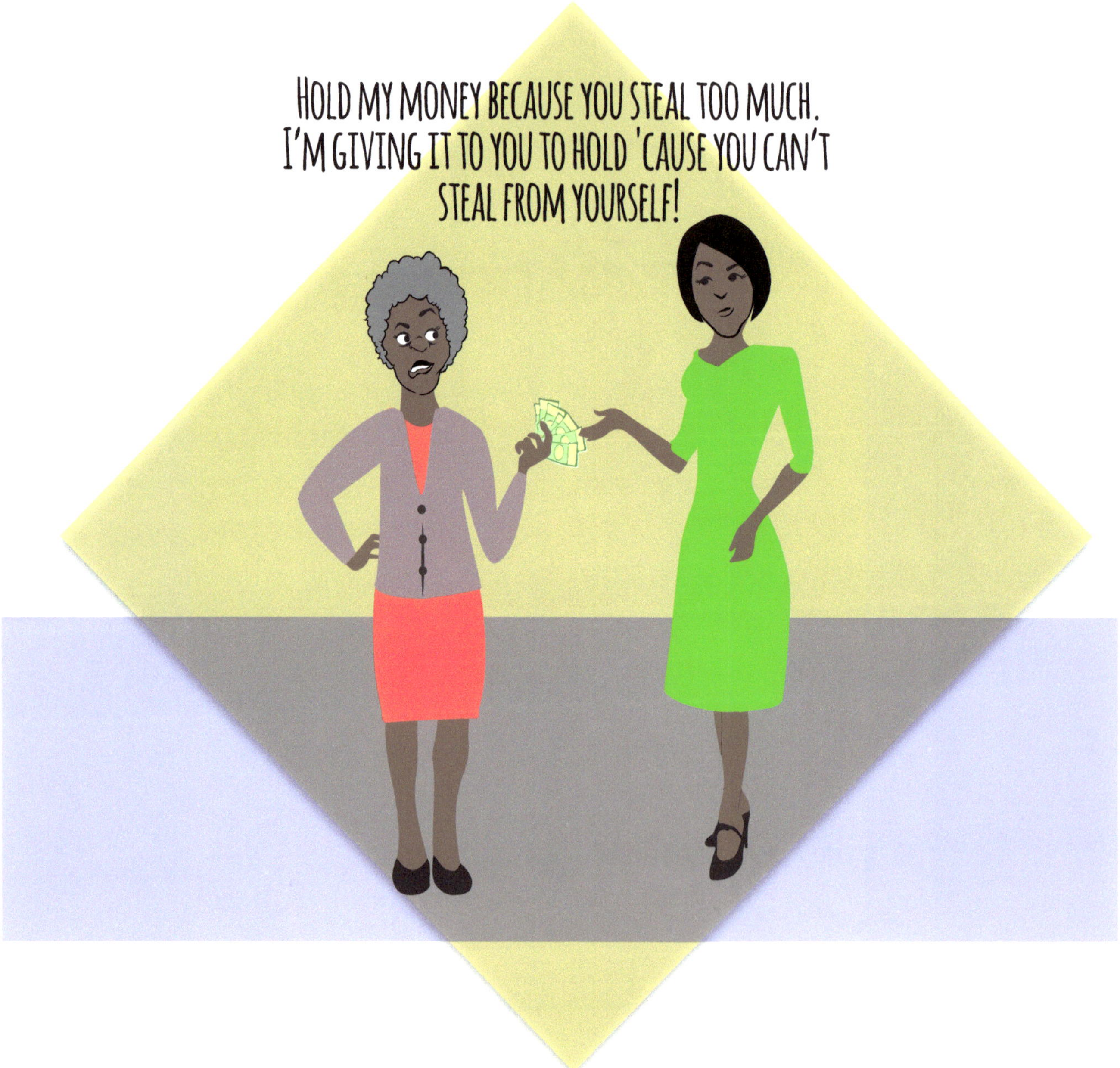

CAN'T STEAL FROM YOURSELF

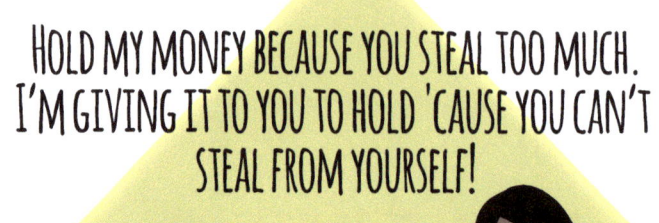

GIMME MY MONEY

WANNA GO HOME

HUSH YO' MOUTH

I ain't never been one to talk to a lot of people. What I got to talk about so much? After a while, you run out of stuff to talk about, and you start lying.

CRUSTY FEET

I ALWAYS HAD NICE FEET. I AIN'T NEVER HAD NO CRUSTS. BUT I'M GETTING OLDER NOW.

DEAD LEG

When I asked the doctor what was wrong with my leg 'cause it's all polka-dotted and shedding, he said it's dead skin. I said, "Doctor, look like my whole leg is dead!"

WAKE UP 65

TEETH DON'T FIT

KUNG FU FIGHTING

WHOP THEIR ASS

WEDDING GIFT

Every ten years you gotta get married to get a gift? What's the matter with you?

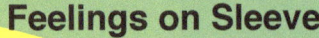**Feelings on Sleeve**

Don't wear your feelings on your sleeve, and they won't be stepped on.

PART 2:
CONVERSATIONS WITH #AUNTALMA

Jesus & Company

Not being able to breathe is no fun, so it's good to have access to the Lord. That's Aunt Alma, and she keeps the Lord busy—very busy. She's got Him on speed dial, which is great—as long as she knows where her phone is, which is rare.

Auntie said she was in pain from struggling to breathe, so she prayed about it, of course. Nothing changed right away. She prayed some more about it. Still, nothing changed. She prayed some more—and harder.

"I couldn't breathe the other day," she told me. "I was feeling so bad, I said, 'Lord! Help me, Lord!' But the pain was still there."

Aunt Alma decided then that Jesus must be too busy. "I called Him, and He must've been busy, so I figured He could send me somebody else—His mommy, His daddy, His cousin, or somebody. I didn't care *who* He sent, as long as I could breathe."

"I know He be busy 'cause a lot of people are calling on Him," she said.

Being the considerate person she is, she thought it generous to allow someone to fill in for Jesus. "I called on Jesus's mother, but she didn't come." Auntie followed that up with calling on His cousin.

"His cousin?" I asked.

"Yeah, John the Baptist." Of course! John the Baptist! What was I thinking?

I know all about having a substitute for a teacher—but a substitute for the Savior? This was a first.

Somebody eventually came to her rescue. I have a feeling none of them really wanted to make the trip to deal with Aunt Alma, but somebody obviously lost the coin toss and showed up because she's still breathing.

JESUS & COMPANY

I couldn't breathe, so I called on Jesus. He must've been busy, so I figured He could send me somebody else—His mommy, His daddy, His cousin, or somebody. I didn't care who He sent, as long as I could breathe.

Ain't Staying in Here

Aunt Alma and I spoke on the phone, and she told me about a phone conversation she had with a friend on a Saturday night. While they enjoyed their talk, she began to feel weird, she said. "It was pain like I was having a heart attack," she described. She told her friend to pray, and she did.

After praying for Auntie, her friend said she should turn over in the bed to the other side, suggesting that my aunt had just been on that side of her body too long.

"I can't turn over," Aunt Alma said.

"Why not?"

"Because I'm already halfway to 111th Avenue! I ain't g'on be in this house having no heart attack!"

Just that fast, my aunt had gotten up, left the house, and had walked quite a ways from home.

"I ain't g'on be in this house having no heart attack! I'm goin' somewhere where there's some people! I'm-a be out walking and swinging my arms!"

Aunt Alma meant it. She said she was going somewhere—anywhere—where there were some people so that if she actually did have a heart attack, somebody would see her and help her.

She may not have known where she was going, but she knew she wanted to be seen.

"I ain't staying up in here!" was all she knew.

I'm not sure how much time transpired until she felt well enough to return to the house, until she was sure she wasn't having a heart attack, but for however long that was, she was outside walking and swinging her arms!

AIN'T STAYING IN HERE

I ain't g'on be in the house having no heart attack! I'm goin' somewhere where there's some people! I'm-a be out walking and swinging my arms!

What Time Is It?

Aunt Alma has many constants: she loses everything, she's always late, she can't remember names, and her car hardly ever runs. Those are just off the top of my head. Another constant, which I would never have known had I not moved away a few years ago, is that she cannot wrap her brain around the time difference between where I live now, Missouri, and where she lives, New York.

So we have the conversation every so often. We have it even more often than we have the discussion about my cat's name. "What's his name again—Trouble?" For the record, he *is* Trouble, with a capital T, but that has nothing to do with his name; it's his personality. His name is Trooper, but Aunt Alma constantly forgets that--just like she forgets the time. Just when I think she's got it...well, she doesn't have it. Okay, that's not true. I actually never think she's got it—not anymore. I know her well enough to know that it's just a matter of time before she asks again what time it is in Missouri—and Lord, help us after we've moved our clocks ahead or back for Daylight or Standard Time changes! By the time I'm done explaining that I'm still just one hour behind, *I'm* ready to fall back or spring ahead away from the discussion!

"We on the same time now?" That's the question I get after a time change. Good luck trying to explain to her that we always have an hour time difference between us.

Our conversations on the subject have been many:

Aunt Alma: Your time is different from my time, right?
Me: Yes, it's 9:44 here. It's 10:44 where you are.
Aunt Alma: No, it ain't. My time got turned back.
Me: Everybody's time got turned back! I'm still one hour behind you.
Aunt Alma: Oh, so it's after 9:00 there and after 10:00 here?
Me: Yes, Auntie!

Four days later, she was back at it:

Aunt Alma: Our time went back a few days ago. Your time went back?
Me (chuckling): Yes, Auntie. It's 9:00 there, and it's 8:00 here.
Aunt Alma: We on the same time now?
Me (shaking my head): No, Auntie. We're still an hour behind you. It's 8:00 here. Where you are, it's 9:00.
Aunt Alma: Oh, so y'all still an hour behind us.
Me: Uh-huh.

One year later, it was time again. As if on cue, here's how the phone conversation at 6:20 p.m. went:

Aunt Alma: Y'all got the same time now at home we got here?
Me (for the 100th time!): No, we're an hour earlier.
Aunt Alma: So it's 7:20 there?
Me: No, it's 5:20.
Aunt Alma: Oh, so it ain't night there yet?

It'll never end.

WHAT TIME IS IT THERE?

We on the same time now?

ATM Auntie

Technology is not my aunt's strength. I'm just glad she can handle a phone—semi-handle one, that is. She manages to handle an ATM also, but not without cries for help.

I was visiting New York for a few days during the Thanksgiving holiday, and Aunt Alma asked me to go with her to the bank so she could use the ATM. I had never seen so many people lined up to use one. But this was New York, of course, and New York always makes a statement. This particular evening, my aunt was making the statement—loudly.

It was cold, so we were clothed in our winter coats. I'm almost always cold, and I guess I get that from her, but she's ten times worse. It's normal to find her in a hat, coat, gloves, and scarf when others are fanning themselves. This day, the winter clothing was merited, and she was as loud at that ATM inside the bank as the winter wind was outside.

I went to the machine with her and talked her through the prompts, starting with the PIN number. Most of us are aware that our PINs are not for public consumption and no one else should hear it, but she must have missed that memo. As she tapped in her PIN, she announced it loudly, "PIN 4325." As if that weren't bad enough, when the ATM prompted her for the amount she wanted to withdraw, in the presence of the crowd, she said loudly, "$500."

Thankfully, we made it out of there without getting robbed, but we still could have gotten hurt. Why? Well, as we turned to leave, Auntie led the way, and I was on her heels, but she headed not toward the door through which we entered, but toward the counter behind which the bank employees work—with her winter scarf masking much of her face! She caught herself before making her move and wondered aloud, "Oh, my! Where am I going? I don't work here. With this scarf 'round my head, too?! I'm go'n get us shot!"

I was never so glad to see the outside of a bank, as cold as it was out there, than I was that day. With Aunt Alma, even a trip to the bank is full of drama.

ATM AUNTIE

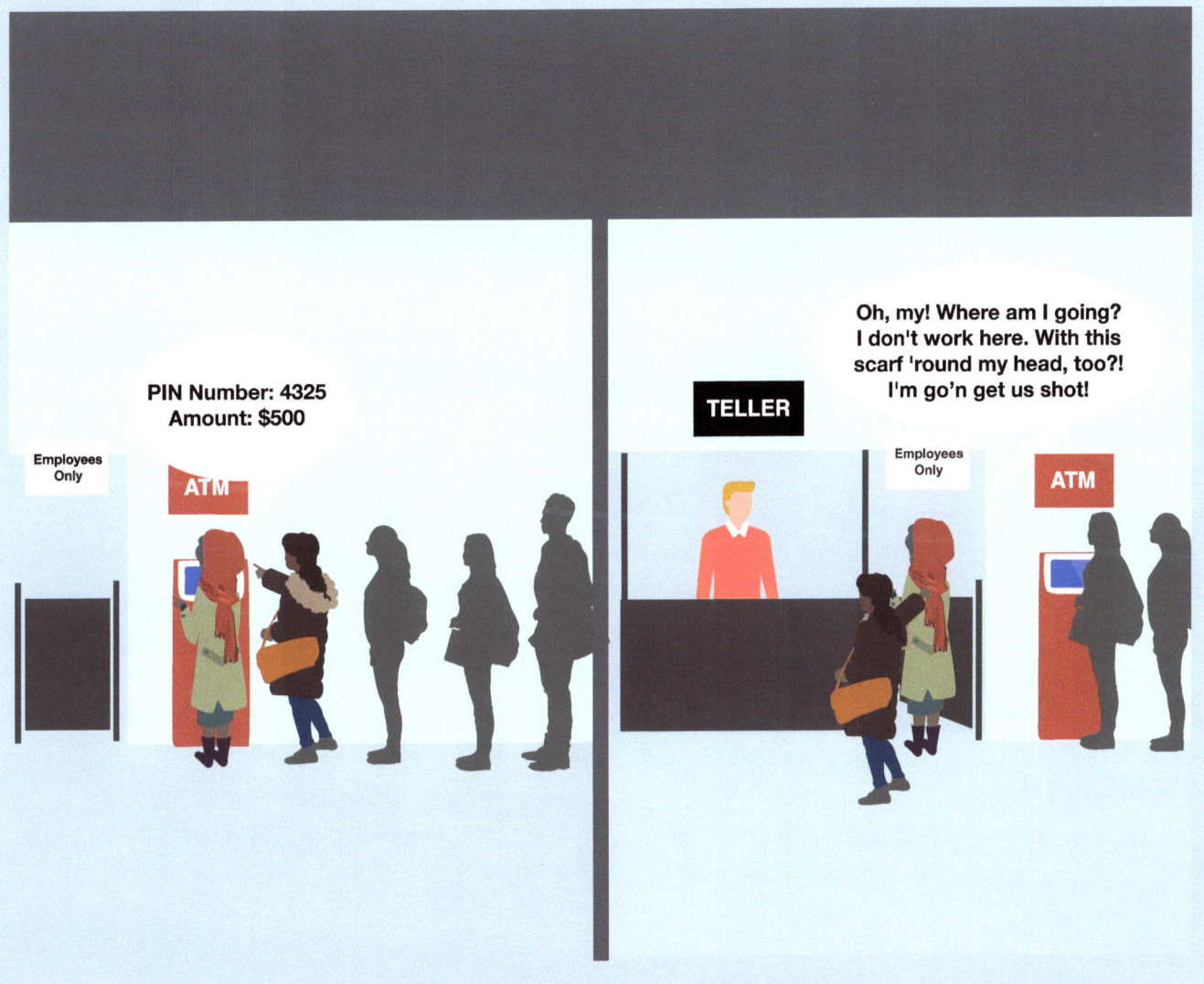

Ain't Scared to Die

If you know my aunt, you know that she is not one to live life on the edge—unless you consider that car of hers. Driving it is always dangerous—and requires great faith. You never know if it'll make it to its destination. Most of the time, it sits in the mechanic's yard. Once it's "fixed," it returns to the mechanic's yard because whatever was wrong with it is rarely ever really fixed. There's not much more danger Auntie will get close to.

Flying on an airplane is not something she wants to do, though she's told me many times that if I needed her, she wouldn't hesitate to hop on a plane. If she must fly, Aunt Alma would prefer to fly with one of her friends from church, who travels a lot.

We spoke on the phone about a conference in New Orleans she was attending the following week. She and this "sister" from church were flying together. Knowing that Aunt Alma was never happy about traveling by plane, she asked my aunt, "You okay about going? You scared?"

Aunt Alma told me she replied, "I ain't never been scared to die with someone I know. Don't I know you?" Then she busted out laughing on the phone. I couldn't help but laugh also. I guess she was expecting to die and was okay with that since she was with her flying friend!

AIN'T SCARED TO DIE

Have Dog, Will Travel

Aunt Alma's two dogs, Tiny and Shirley, are as high-maintenance as she is. They eat special food, suffer from allergies, take medication, and are loved profusely. I've been in the house when she has left. They move the curtains aside so they can look out the window, and while she's gone, they pace the floor, anxious for her return. Because of their various conditions, they occasionally need to go to the vet. But because Auntie's car is usually broken down, she does not always have a way to get them there.

When she can, she gets a friend to take her to the vet, but she doesn't like to do that because, she acknowledged, people don't want hairy dogs in their car. Shirley needed to go to the vet, and the friend who usually wouldn't mind taking my aunt and Shirley wasn't available.

Auntie told me that she wasn't going to worry about not having her car or getting someone to help. If she had to, she said, she would put her dog in a cage and take her on the bus—a New York City bus! She wasn't worried about who gave her the evil eye, either. She loves her dogs too much to be stopped by something so small.

She told me, "I'll put my dog in a cage and get on that bus and go on 'bout my bi'ness."

HAVE DOG, WILL TRAVEL

Dirty Glasses

Some people have plans that include going for a walk, calling a loved one, drinking eight glasses of water. Aunt Alma's plans involve harassing her doctors. Let the slightest thing be off, and she's there. She used to call them first and try to set up an appointment to get in. I guess she found that doctors, who tell her that she's healthier than she thinks she is, were able to dissuade her from coming in, so now, she doesn't bother to call; she just shows up. In fact, she does her best to get there before the office opens. The first thing the doctor sees when he gets there is my aunt waving at him. I just know he's thinking, "Oh, no! Not again! Help me, Lord!"

Her trip to the doctor has now extended beyond the various medical doctors she sees. She recently found herself in the eye doctor's office. She said her vision just wasn't clear enough. She was having problems, and she wanted answers. After tests, the conversation went like this:

Aunt Alma: Doctor, something is wrong. I can't see out my eyes!
Doctor: There's nothing wrong with your eyes. All your tests came back fine—but you might want to clean your glasses.

It turns out her glasses were just dirty, smudged. She had been ready to ask for some kind of surgical procedure!

God bless the doctors who take care of Aunt Alma's body—from her eyes to her feet—because they sure do have their hands full!

DIRTY GLASSES

Fainting Auntie

I'm a cold-natured kind of gal. I am often freezing when others are not even cold. I like to have the heat turned up so that I'm not the least bit chilled. Maybe I get it from Aunt Alma. She's ten times worse than I am, however. When everyone—including me—is burning up, she'll have the heat on in the house, set to 80 degrees or higher. Then she'll go on some errand dressed like it's winter, though it's scorching.

Wearing a coat, hat, and boots, she headed out the door to walk her dogs one day. Her comment as she left the house was, "I'll probably faint out here, wearing this coat and hat."

"Yes, and the rest of us will probably faint, too, as we watch you in that coat and hat!" I wanted to say.

Well, at least she recognized that it was hot. Recognizing it didn't make her take off her winter gear, but it's still comforting to know she felt the heat. There is hope yet!

Shirley and Tiny survived their walk, but they were panting for breath along the way.

FAINTING AUNTIE

Some Like It Hot

Aunt Alma's love affair with the heat is never-ending. I was visiting her in mid-June, and it was blistering in the house. I sat on the dining room floor in front of a fan and fanned myself also—willing to do any and everything to get cool.

Aunt Alma came into the dining room and said, "I'm going to turn the heat off."

The heat off? It was not even 10:00 a.m., already almost 80 degrees, and she had the heat on? All I could muster was just that: "You have the heat on?"

Her answer: "Uh-huh." Meanwhile, I was still sitting in front of the fan.

Mind you, the day before, when it was 84 degrees, she suggested I borrow one of her sweaters if I needed it. I have no idea what gave her the impression that I needed a sweater. I was sitting in front of the fan then also, but she didn't notice. "You might want to put on a jacket or borrow one of my sweaters," she said.

SOME LIKE IT HOT

Feel It in My Bones

"I didn't dance, but I know I could've. I could feel it in my bones!"

This was Aunt Alma's summary of a friend's birthday party she attended. Her 80-year-old friend! Hold up. Why are we surprised? What makes us think old folks can't party? Young folks don't hold the patent on getting down!

I guess Aunt Alma had such a good time feeling the beat from her seat she didn't need to get out on the dance floor, but she was dancing on the inside. She was groovin' in ways nobody could see!

She had a good time at that party. I bet next time she'll get out on the dance floor, probably at her own party—**when she turns 100!**

FEEL IT IN MY BONES

Ain't No Peanuts

Any Christmas morning that includes Aunt Alma is an adventure. With her, every single day is a trip. This particular Christmas, I was awakened before 7:00 a.m. when my phone rang.

On the other end was Aunt Alma's typical loud voice. Immediately, she started ranting about a box I sent to her house with presents for her and my siblings. The family sends all packages to her house. She often says that my brother, Andrew, and my sister, Marion, whom we call Mona, always order things and have them sent to her house as if she is supposed to hang around the house all day waiting for the delivery man. I guess I'm no better because I sent everyone's Christmas gift in one big box to Aunt Alma's house that year.

Upon answering the phone, I heard her voice—much too loud—saying that my sister's gift was not in the box.

I knew the gift was in there because I put it in there myself. So I just stopped her and said, "Merry Christmas" because she hadn't said it to me; she just lit right in about the box. I was half-asleep, she was all loud, and I knew the gift was in the box, so I said, "It's under the peanuts."

After a second, she said, "There ain't no peanuts in this box!"

I said, "The *packing* peanuts!" Oy vey!

I told her she was loud and that it was too early for all that.

"It's not even 7:00," I added.

"It's almost 8:00 here," she said. I told her it was not 8:00 where I lived and asked her to tone it down.

She responded, "Well, A-dri-enne (with an attitude), it's 8:00 here!"

She then basically said that she was operating on her own time zone.

Laughing, though not overly amused at that point, I said, "That would be fine if you were calling yourself!"

Then, still loud, she had the nerve to rush me off the phone because, she announced, she was running late for church—as if I called her instead of her calling me!

I'd like to think that she will search the box fully next time before she calls me to tell me the gift that I know I put in there is not in there. I also would like to think that now she knows the difference between peanuts that people eat and peanuts that people use to protect items we pack and send off.

AIN'T NO PEANUTS

Ain't no peanuts in this box!

Can't Count

It's not just *time* Aunt Alma is bad at. Maybe she struggles with *all* numbers. We had an interesting conversation during one of my visits to New York. All I could do was shake my head.

As we were in the kitchen, she suddenly realized something:

Aunt Alma: "I'm running behind in getting my breakfast. It's 8:00?"
Me: I told you it was 8:00 eleven minutes ago.
Aunt Alma: So it's 8:30?

Like I said, maybe it's *all* numbers.

CAN'T COUNT

Keep On Truckin'

Aunt Alma was definitely not about to ride long-distance with her old friend. It sounded to me like a good time, but Aunt Alma did not hear it the way I heard it. She heard disaster, or possible-disaster, which, to her, was the same thing.

This friend had been visiting New York and invited my aunt to accompany her back to Georgia on the road trip. It would be a chance for the two to catch up and for my aunt to have a little vacation in Georgia. Auntie could not get past the idea of being on the road for such a long drive with someone so far along in years.

"*I'm* bad enough under the wheel," she told her friend. "I don't need to be with *you* under the wheel. Talking 'bout you 90—and I'm go'n ride with you to Georgia? With all them big trucks? Not me!"

Well, I guess she had a point. Did she change her mind? Nope! I'm sure she was pleased to have been invited, but if sharing the highway with a truck was part of the picture, it would have to be taken without her. So she let her friend truck on and decided to keep on trucking herself.

KEEP ON TRUCKIN'

Short & Sweet

It was time to head to the airport. My visit had come to an end, and Aunt Alma was doing the honors of seeing me off.

I divided my time between being Upstate and down in New York City with her, and I was also working. This all made my visit seem even shorter than it was. I thought she had felt the same, but hey, Auntie is practical.

As we got in the car and were about to travel to the airport, she took my hand and said she enjoyed me during my time there. I said it was too short. Of course, I expected agreement. Instead, she said, "That's what makes it good. Short and sweet."

Then, laughing, she explained, "Stay too long, we start getting on each other's nerves!"

If that doesn't keep me humble, nothing will!

SHORT & SWEET

Bingo, Anyone?

Do people still play Bingo? In Aunt Alma's world, they do. In fact, she plans to mesh that classic game with modern technology. The meshing is nothing new to most, but it has only entered my aunt's world by way of imagination; she has yet to embrace modern technology. The cell phone is difficult enough. Bingo on a computer might be just too much.

Nonetheless, every few months, Aunt Alma again entertains the idea of getting a computer.

She told me, "I'm thinking 'bout getting me a computer."

Here we go again. I have often considered getting her a laptop, but she won't even make use of the microwave and blender I got her. They just sit there, so I wondered again why she wanted a computer. "What you gonna do with a computer?" I asked.

"Play me a game or something," she announced. "I'm go'n get me a partner and play Bingo."

I'd love to see that. For now, she still has no computer, and she still has her hands full just trying to operate her cell phone.

BINGO, ANYONE?

Swipe It

Aunt Alma is quick to tell you how she's growing old and spending lots of time at doctors' appointments. I tease that for someone whose legs are always bothering her, she sure gets around. You can hardly keep up with her. I call, and she's out and about somewhere. When I'm there, she's walking out as I'm walking in. Oh yeah, she keeps it moving.

I hadn't been able to reach her for several days, though I had left voicemails. Now, that was somewhat par for the course, especially because, for the longest time, she didn't know how to access voicemails. We had taken care of that, though. She got a new cell phone a few weeks prior—a touchscreen—and I showed her how to answer, dial, and check her voicemail. So I really should have heard back from her this time, but I had not.

When she finally called me, she told me that she had the new touchscreen to deal with. She added that she didn't know how to use it. I reminded her that I had shown her how to answer, dial, and check her messages. She responded, "I knew how to do those things for only about an hour!" She said it had taken 100 attempts before she was able to connect to me that night.

That wasn't the only problem. She told me her phone service was just turned back on. I was confused, so she explained. It seems her service provider had turned it off after several calls to various countries were made from it, including the country of "Matamala."

That must be a new country.

Those calls to "Matamala"—and other renamed nations!—made the company suspect that someone had stolen her phone and was calling all over the world.

Needless to say, Aunt Alma's new touchscreen didn't make the cut. She returned it, and the store gave her an old-school one in its place, but it didn't take long for her to destroy it. Don't be surprised. After all, we're talking about Aunt Alma.

Not long after, I wasn't able to contact her. I had to get through to her on the house phone instead. I asked her where her cell phone was, and we had the following conversation:

Aunt Alma: I ain't got no phone. It broke.
Me: When are you getting another one?
Aunt Alma: I can't get no 'nother one.
Me: Why?
Aunt Alma: They don't got no more of them machines with 1, 2, 3 on it. And I can't swipe no phone. I tried that before, remember?

Yes, I remember. We all remember—even the citizens of "Matamala."

SWIPE IT

They don't got no more of them machines with 1, 2, 3 on it. And I can't swipe no phone.

Let Me Count the Waves

Get a new television? Aunt Alma? Be serious! She'd sooner get a new vehicle than a new TV, and that's not about to happen, though that car spends more time at the mechanic's shop than Auntie spends at the doctor's office.

She was in her bedroom trying to get her raggedy television to work. It was cutting off and on as it saw fit. When I asked her why, she had the perfect explanation.

"The waves have to come through the window," Aunt Alma said as if her words made perfect sense. She stood in front of the window, beckoning the waves with her arms.

Ignoring the waves, the television turned itself off again. Unfazed, my aunt knew what to do.

"Let me open up this window," she said, and she did. I guess the waves have easier access when they don't have to force their way through a closed window.

I left Auntie to her own devices and retreated to another room. The open window must have done the trick, though, because I soon heard her ask her dogs, "What time does *Judge Judy* come on?"

They did not answer.

No Time for "Hello"

"Hello," I said as I answered the phone that morning.

"What's your new address?" asked the voice on the other end. It was Aunt Alma.

"Hello," I repeated.

"I need your new address," she said.

"Hello."

She then asked if I could hear her. Of course, I could. So why was I repeating "hello" instead of giving her my address? Simple. I was waiting for my "hello," and it hadn't come yet. So I told her that I didn't answer questions before I got a "hello."

Her response? "I ain't got time for no 'hello.'" She was at the post office, she said, needed my address quickly so she could send me a package, and I needed to hurry up and tell her.

Maybe it's just me, but I thought that in the time it took her to tell me why she didn't have time to tell me "hello," she could have told me "hello"! But what do I know? She's the aunt. I'm the niece. So I did what I was told: I gave her my address. "Goodbye," she then said—and hung up.

NO TIME FOR "HELLO"

Put It in the Bowl

Periodically, my aunt likes to go to a popular sandwich eatery and treat herself to lunch. Then she learned that the establishment puts the same chemicals in its bread that goes into yoga mats and shoes. Armed with a Plan B, she went there with a bowl and shoved it toward the man behind the counter.

Understandably, the man was confused—but not for long. She told him what meat and veggies she wanted and demanded, "Put it in this bowl. I'll go home and put it on my own bread!"

This was probably the first such request this guy had ever gotten, and he did not know how to react. Auntie made it plain. "I don't want your bread. I'll use my own," she told him.

He did as he was told.

PUT IT IN THE BOWL

Bilingual Dogs

It's not enough for Auntie's dogs, Shirley and Tiny, to have food, water, and toys when she has to leave them to run errands. Aunt Alma goes beyond that. She leaves the television on, too, for their entertainment.

I observed her preparing to leave the house. She put on her coat and hat and was holding her purse. The dogs were by her side, sensing, I'm sure, that she was heading out. As sound from the television filled the room, I noticed that what was coming from the television was not our native language.

"Aunt Alma," I said, "that's Spanish. Why do you have it on a Spanish channel?"

She responded, "It's for the dogs. They don't know it's Spanish!"

Leave it to Auntie. They don't know it's Spanish, but somehow they know to watch it. And if they don't know it's Spanish, why select a Spanish channel? Well, they *are* smart. It's possible that some of the language could rub off on them. Maybe Aunt Alma will end up with bilingual dogs.

BILINGUAL DOGS

It's for the dogs. They don't know it's Spanish!

MEET THE AUTHOR

ADRIENNE ROSS is an author, editor, columnist, speaker, and former teacher and coach. She owns Adrienne Ross Communications and speaks at schools, churches, political events, and national and international service organization conferences. Humor is a significant part of her presentations, as she believes that without laughter, there is no inspiration.

Adrienne is the author of *#AuntAlma: Raisin' a Little ~~Hell~~ Heaven on Earth*, the first of the *#AuntAlma* books, and the inspirational *Push Your Way to Purpose: How to Get from Where You Are to Where You're Meant to Be*.

Contact her at adriennerosscom.com and auntalma.com.

CONTACT THE AUTHOR

To schedule Adrienne Ross to speak
at your event or purchase her books in bulk:

adriennerosscom.com

auntalma.com

adriennerosscom@gmail.com

www.ingramcontent.com/pod-product-compliance
Lightning Source LLC
Chambersburg PA
CBHW041700160426
43191CB00002B/33